It Wasn't the
Badge,

It Was the
Grace of
God

REV. GARY A. JONES

authorHOUSE®

AuthorHouse™
1663 Liberty Drive
Bloomington, IN 47403
www.authorhouse.com
Phone: 833-262-8899

Published by AuthorHouse 02/17/2021

ISBN: 978-1-6655-1736-2 (sc)
ISBN: 978-1-6655-1735-5 (e)

Library of Congress Control Number: 2021903324

Print information available on the last page.

This book is printed on acid-free paper.

DEDICATIONS

This book is dedicated to the people that I hold most dear to my life. These are the people that I feel have made the most impact on my life and the direction that my life has gone in.

First of all, I want to acknowledge all of my partners on the Detroit Police Department, especially the **Narcotics Street Enforcement Unit.** We have a logo that says, "Street For Life" or S4L. I love you all with all my heart!

One of my best friends, Anthony Williams. Anthony and I, along with Ricky Brown, were best friends that decided to join the Detroit Police Department together. Anthony was a very strong willed man, who would always step up to the challenges of life. Anthony was 27 years old when he was killed in the line of duty while being a hero and saving the lives of many others.

Next is the man that I say is my only earthly hero. My ultimate hero is Jesus Christ, my Lord and Savior, but this man is my dad, the late Horace Edsel Jones. My dad was a hard working family man, who taught me how to be a man. He taught me the true values in life; God, family and hard work. He taught me that life holds no promises but God's word would get me through this life's ups and downs. He was a strong man, worked hard and took care of his family.

My mother is next, Daisy Mentoria Jones. My Queen, the lady of my life. Strong, opinionated, fun loving, hardworking and God fearing. She raise her five children and when we were able to take care of ourselves, she went to work. When dad became ill, she neglected her own health to take care of him. She was always concerned about me as a Police Officer and prayed daily for my protection. She was not just mom, but she was my very best friend who I could talk to about everything!

My Children, Damien Jones, Brandon Jones and Ashlei Jones. They are my joy and I thank God for these three angels!

Last but certainly not least is my wife, Nettie M. Jones. As of this writing, we have been married for 24 years. It has not been an easy 24 years for her. I have put her through hell. My promiscuity, which she had every right to leave me for early on in our marriage. My gambling, which put us into ruin, my illnesses, a stroke that should have left me a cripple, not able to walk or talk but by the grace of God, and then the amputation of part of my right leg, where I had to depend on her to get me around and help me to recover. She is God sent and my love for her is without measure!

INTRODUCTION

This book was originally going to be a collection of stories about Police Officers and how God brought them through certain situations or how He used them for what they were called to do, protect and serve. God, however, had other plans for me. After I got no response from other law enforcement officers, I went to the Lord in prayer to find out what was wrong. I already knew that I was to write this book, but there was something I was missing. God answered me right away and said that the book is a good idea, but my own personal account would be enough to say what needs to be said.

What needs to be said in this day and age is that the police are over all good. That the police are the chosen few, called on by God to be the protectors of the land. To be the friends of the people, not just enforcers of the law, but good will ambassadors, there to help, to direct, to guide, to talk to and confide in. There to bring peace and to keep peace. Called by God to be there for the people of the land, not against them. For all the people, no matter where they come from, how they look or what language they speak. Called to serve God's people.

I was called to minister to God's people which was a more definitive calling, but this calling was one that I could not explain so clearly. Oh, it was a calling for sure, but I could not explain it to you at the time. I had just turned nineteen years old when I started the Detroit Police Academy in 1977. The late Coleman Young was Major of the city and had implemented the affirmative action plan in Detroit to hire more minorities into city services, namely police, fire and EMS. My friends and I thought it would be a good idea to put in some applications. It was myself, Anthony Williams, Ricky Brown and David Lee. David could not continue because of medical reasons. The three of us, however, pushed on. We applied for the police and the fire departments. We were actually call by the fire department first, but while sitting down over a few beers we decided that we would rather take our chances with being shot rather than being burned. So we harassed our recruiter, Sgt. Broadnax, until he was convince that we were for real in wanted to pursue this endeavor.

So I completed the academy and was assigned to the thirteenth precinct. It was all new and different, being in a place in Detroit that I had absolutely no knowledge of. Walking a beat in one of the most dangerous areas in the city on the afternoon shift with two other rookie female officers. Challenges arose daily, but God saw me through them all. There will be a few stories associated with my time in the thirteenth precinct, but what I want to focus on mostly is God's mercy and grace and how He put me where I needed to be or took me away from the what could have been harmful to me.

God had called me to this position for very specific reasons. These reasons were not apparent until they came to past, but it was very clear to me that this was God, LOUD AND CLEAR! The job of law enforcement is something only a select few can do. There are many in the position for the wrong reasons; pride, glory, racism, greed, to carry a gun legally, to wear the uniform and to justify their abusive treatment of others. These people are far and in between. The majority of all law enforcement are there to do God's will. Called by God to, again, SERVE THE PEOPLE OF GOD!

I pray that you will read theses short stories of mine, first as an example of what we go through as police officers, and second to understand and appreciate how we put our lives on the line every day to make sure that you can live in God's peace.

SHOTGUN TESTIMONY

John 14:26 (KJV) But the Comforter, which is the Holy Ghost, whom the Father will send in my name, he shall teach you all things, and bring all things to your remembrance, whatsoever I have said unto you.

This story was at first going to be at the end or at least in the middle of this writing. The LORD spoke to me, however, and said that this story needed to be the starting point of this writing. See, this story is where I believe my salvation started. There will be stories that came before it and others that will follow it, but this is where I know the Holy Spirit was first realize to be in me, by me.

I joined the Detroit Police Department's "Narcotics Street Enforcement Unit", around 1988. We were a special unit, designed to combat the new high level of street corner narcotic sells (first of its kind in the country). We had gone far beyond just the street corners however. Much of what we uncovered on the streets lead to more illegal narcotic activities in buildings and the mail and all sorts of venues used in the illegal sell of drugs. The Narcotics Street

Enforcement Unit (NSEU) had become multi-functional very quickly.

On this particular day, we were conducting a raid on a single family home on the west side of the city. As I recall, it was in the 12th precinct, in the area of W. Outer Drive and Meyers. The succession of entry was as follows; first the Ram man, who forced the door open as we announce our presence. Next the Shotgun man, who cleared each room of any occupants and forced them back to the rest of the team. In his shadow was his Backup man, who went with the Shotgun man's every move to serve as just that, his backup!

On this particular day, I was this Backup man and my best friend in life, Ricky Brown, was the Shotgun man. Now Ricky and I had known each other and had immediately become best friends since day one of the 7th grade, and we still are! We had become very proficient in conducting these raids. We were very precise and systematic in what we did. We started clearing the house, forcing occupants back to the rest of the team. We came upon a narrow hallway, where there was a locked door right in the middle of the hallway.

This is where it gets interesting. Rick decides that he would force this door open by hitting it with the butt of the shotgun. A voice said to me, "duck"! I am thinking, so that I can see around Rick as the door opens. Notice, I didn't say to myself to duck, it was a voice. I heard this voice loud and clear, but it was a voice inside of me, one that no one else could hear. As I bent down, Rick hit the door, and the shot gun went off! The shotgun went off right over my head from two feet away! Where did this voice come from? I didn't know. But we celebrated another successful raid, uncovered a lot of drugs, made some good felony arrest and everyone went to the bar. Night after night, however, I continued to ponder the question, where did that voice come from?

Now I had given my life to Christ a long time before this, when I was just a teenager, but I had not lived a life as a Christian. There was always something burning inside of me. I heard voices often and was afraid that people would think I was crazy or something. But this time it got me to thinking about God! Had I not listened to the voice and did what it said to do, where would I be? What would have happened? Was this a sign from God? Was this His voice? Why was He saving me? Lives were saved that day beyond mine. Ricky Brown would have killed his best friend, the rest of the crew would have be devastated and probably no longer continue. Most of all I would be dead!

I have learned that this voice that has been with me all of my life, is the voice of what is inside of us all, it is the voice of the Holy Spirit, that lives in us all. Through God's mercy and grace, we have been given favor, favor to live free of the thing which we subject ourselves to everyday. We should all be dead, because we are all sinners, born in sin because

3

of one man's disobedience, yet we are saved because of one Man's obedience. Adam's disobedience caused us all to be sinners. Born that way without having to do anything. But Jesus Christ died for our sins so that we can be born again without sin! **John 3:16,** *For God so loved the world, that He gave his only begotten Son, that whosoever believeth in him should not perish, but have everlasting life. (KJV)*

I have a sister, Kim, who lives in New York. During 9/11, Kim was employed by...... and working on the ..... floor. Kim was working that day, but the Holy Spirit spoke to her and she is alive today because she listened, reluctantly, but she listened. Have you ever had an occasion when you just knew you should have followed your "first mind"? "I knew I should not have gone this way", or "something told me to do it this way or that way". "If I had listened to my first mind, I wouldn't be in this trouble", or "I am so glad I went with my first thought". Sometimes that first thought, and I should say often times, is the Holy Spirit talking to you to guide you to or away from something. It could mean the difference between being prosperous or broke, getting that new job or allowing someone else to get it. The Holy Spirit or the Holy Ghost is here to comfort us, to guide us, to protect us.

On 9/11 ...... as I entered my job location, late. I observed everyone gathered around the television in utter amazement. As I got closer to see what the fuss was all about, I observed the second plane going into the twin towers. I thought that this had to be a movie or something, until someone said to me that this was live! I screamed while running out the room, "this can't be live, my sister in in there". I have two other sisters and a brother, all in Detroit. We all gathered together at other childhood home and began to pray. Praying and crying, we all had a feeling that something was going on with Kim, that we couldn't lose hope.

Kim happens to be a twin to our sister Karen. Karen was very upset because she and Kim talked every night on the phone, but had not talked that night before. At about 1:30pm, the phone rang, and glory be to God it was Kim. The day before 9/11, Kim's boss begged her to go to …… for him. Kim did not want to go but the Holy Spirit insisted! Kim listened, not so much to her boss, it was not an order, it was a favor, but the insistent voice of the Holy Spirit that told her to go! She rushed off to the airport that night, not having time to call her sister, and her life was saved!

Do not be afraid to follow your first mind, it usually is the mind of the Holy Spirit, who was sent here to help us, to guide us to protect us. He moved me out of the way of a bullet and moved my sister out of the way of a terrorist. We heard Him speak and we did what was told to us to do.

DEATH AND LIFE

Isaiah 25: 8: He will shallow up death in victory; and the LORD GOD will wipe away tears from off all faces; and the rebuke of his people shall he take away from off all the earth; for the LORD hath spoken it. (KJV)

I was prepared by God at an early age to be able to deal with death, violent death. I was working as a security guard at the Wonder Bread factory in Detroit. It is now the Motor City Casino. I was given a ten speed bicycle to patrol the exterior of the building. Early one morning as I rode into the dock area, I noticed a vehicle parked in the alley. As I approached the car, I noticed that someone was leaning out of the driver's side door. I was thinking someone may have been drunk. I rode my bike up to the individual to find that He was and elderly white man who had been shot on the head and his brain matter was all over the ground. This was my third day at work and not what I had expected to witness. It did not bother me, I called it in and stood by until the police arrived.

As I became a Police Officer, Working in the thirteenth precinct, I continued to witness death in all kinds of ways, some violent, some accidental and some natural. It would appear that on an average week, I would see at least five to ten deaths. Early one Saturday morning, I received a police run to a hotel where there was an apparent overdose of a well-known prostitute. While conducting my investigation and making the proper notifications (homicide unit, EMS, etc.), an elderly gentleman walked in carrying some breakfast food from the restaurant. He was perplexed to see the police in his room. When I asked him what he knew about the lady, he explained that she was his date. When I asked him for identification, I was perplexed myself to find that this man was a very well-known and popular Baptist Pastor of a well-known Baptist church and the dead prostitute was not his wife!

God has an amazing way of bringing the truth to light! You can think that you are getting away from it, hiding from it or being deceitful about it, but God sees all and knows all. The flesh is weak to all men no matter what your status. The Scripture reads in **Matt. 26:41- Watch and pray, that ye not enter into temptation: the spirit indeed is willing, but the flesh is weak. (KJV)**

I have seen so many deaths that I cannot count them. But as many deaths that I saw, I saw and able to save a few lives that outweighed the many deaths. One incident that will always stick with me was on a street named Oakland. I and my partner that day, Jessie, were on routine patrol when we noticed a young man standing in the street near the curb, pointing a hand gun at another young man and a young lady. There was also a little boy standing in the street with a very large butcher's knife in his hand. I was the driver and stopped the scout car just short of this scene. Jessie and I exited the scout car, screaming to the young man to drop the weapon, while pointing our guns at him.

The young man, while shaking and beginning to cry, started saying that he had enough and couldn't take any more. I asked him to calm down and tell me what the problem was, while continuing to point our weapons at him. He began to explain that the young lady was his sister and she was seven months pregnant. The young man with her was her ex-boyfriend, who had just beat her up and drug her out of the house. She was a bloody mess! This had to stop and he was doing what he had to do to save his sister. The other little boy with the knife was his little brother. Their father was nowhere to be found for years and mother was at home strung out on drugs. He was trying to keep his family together. I told him to let the law handle it and that I would make sure that justice was served. I holstered my weapon and told Jessie to keep his weapon out and pointed at him. I told the young man that I understood and would help him, but if he shot the guy then we would have to shoot him.

I walked up behind the young man, put one hand on his shoulder, while sliding the other hand down his arm to meet the gun he was holding. I reached the gun, put my thumb in front of the hammer, and took the gun out of his hands. He collapsed into my arms, crying and saying, "please help me". Jessie took the knife from the little brother. We then arrested the young man with the gun and the young man he was about to kill. All were transported to the precinct and the young lady, to the hospital.

The next day I was at court to sign arrest warrants on both men. I was asked by the judge what the story was. After explaining it to the judge, I asked him if there was something that could be done to save this young man's life. The judge agreed that he was a victim of circumstances and that he needed help. He was charged with a misdemeanor and was given time served. His sentence other than that was he had to report to me on a weekly basis at the precinct to show me his progress. He did just that for several months. He got a job as a security guard and soon after, entered the Police Academy.

I had no idea that this incident happened in front of a church. The little church was having choir rehearsal and stepped outside to see what was going on. The choir went down to the precinct to tell what they saw and wanted to commend me for what I did. Here is where I learned what God meant when He said to be humble. **Matt.**

18:4 – Whosoever therefore shall humble himself as this little child, the same is greatest in the kingdom of heaven. (KJV) My report was given to a very good friend of mine, Sgt. Woodrow Seay, to write me up for a commendation. Sgt. Seay was an avid fisherman and we often talked about going fishing together. The following weekend after this incident, Woodrow invited me to go fishing with him. I told him that I had a prior commitment but I would catch him the next time. Unfortunately there would be no next time. That day Sgt. Seay was involved in a boating accident and was drowned. All of his reports and other paperwork were thrown out, including my commendation. The lord spoke to me again and told me, "I know of thy deeds, your reward is with Me in heaven". So I knew to be humble, I never inquired about the commendation and never looked up the young man who started the police academy. God took care of us both. Woodrow's death was, among all other things that only God knows and has control of, to teach me how to humble myself.

I found that God allowed me to witness so many deaths so as to prepare me to handle death that was close to me. My father had become very ill and had to have 24 hour care. My mother was that care giver, she spent every day and all of her energy in taking care of her husband. One day she called me up to say she was mad at me. When I asked why, she explained that she had not spoken to or seen me in quite some time and she was worried. I made a deal with her that day, that every Saturday morning from now on, I would come over and we would have coffee together and catch up with each other, The second Saturday after that, March 16, 1991, I came over to the house to have our coffee. The night before I stopped by the house and Mom was sitting in the kitchen looking sad. I asked her what the problem was, and she said "I am just a little tired". So I made her get up and go to bed. I kissed her good night and said I will see you in the morning. As I entered the house that morning, I could see into my mother's room. She was fast asleep and my cousin's little girl, Tiffany was asleep with her. Tiffany joined me in the kitchen as I put the coffee pot on. Then God said to me, "Go get your mother". I went back to her room, and as I stepped into the doorway, I could feel a very familiar thing. It was the cold air of death! Mom's lips were blue and Riga mores had set in. My sister was there in her room asleep and Dad was in the back room asleep. It was meant for me to be there because I was "trained" to deal with this. I sat there for a few minutes and talked to her, then I got on the phone to make the proper notifications. I went into my sister's room to wake her and give her the news, and then I did the same with dad. I called my other sisters and my brother to let them know that God had called mom home.

A great side story developed here. The EMS techs arrived and this beautiful woman tech stepped out the truck and said, "Hey, I know you". Earlier in my career, I received a police call early one Sunday morning on a possible crib death. This baby's father woke and found his six week old baby unresponsive. The mother had gotten up and rushed off to church. This same EMS tech showed up, picked that baby up, wrapped it in a blanket and put some makeup on him to make it look like he was just asleep. When the mother arrived, hysterical, the Tech calmed her down and without letting the mother touch the little cold baby, she let her see her baby, sleeping!

This same Tech was the lady that responded to my mother's death. She came in, helped me to dress mom in her robe, combed her hair and made up her face. God's angel was again in my mist. God knows exactly what we need and who we need in our lives at the right time.

God continued to call me to be in places where I was able to prepare others that may not have been able to handle it otherwise. We were preparing for dad's death when mom passed away. Four years after mom's death, I was visiting dad in the hospital. He had been there for quite a while and was not getting better. His lungs were shot, he continued to have mini heart attacks and life was slowing leaving his body. It was September 1, 1995 and dad was not looking too good. To get a smile out of him, I told him that he looked like an octopus with all the tubes coming from him. I got a big smile out of him and then he called me closer so that he could speak to me. He told me that it was time for him to go, but that I should not worry, because God had him. He told me that he only had two regrets in his life. You see, dad had gone blind from his complications with diabetes. He said that his only regrets were that he could not see his wife when she was laid to rest, and that he could not see his granddaughter, my daughter, Ashlei. He was blind by the time she was born and I was the only child to give my parents any grandchildren. He was able to see the first two, my sons Damien and Brandon. But praises be to God, he can see them all right now! The next day, while celebrating Labor Day with my children and my Fiancée, my present wife Nettie, I was called to the hospital, dad had expired that morning.

God called me again to a death of someone very close to me. I had acquired a rental property and was renting to a very nice elderly man, Mr. Garrett. Mr. Garrett had a son who lived directly behind him, but only came to see his dad on the first of the month, when dad got his social security check. He also had a daughter who lived 20 – 30 miles away. Mr. Garrett and I became very close, he was like a father to me. I called him one evening to let him know I would be over the next morning to collect the rent. Mr. Garrett would call me to remind me to come get the rent every month if I did not come on time. This evening He said to me that he was tired and would not be there in the morning. I told him to stop talking like that and that when I arrived in the morning, we would have breakfast together. As I arrived and let myself in, as I always did, I called out to him. I got no answer and I continued to call his name as I entered his bedroom. He was lying in his bed, clothing still on, and he had died, apparently quite some time ago. Again, I stepped into the police mode, made the proper notifications, found his phone and called his daughter, and thanked God for allowing me to be there that morning. **1 Corinthians 15: 20-26; 20. But now is Christ risen from the dead, and become the firstfruits of them that slept. 21. For since by man came death, by man came also the resurrection of the dead. 22. For as in Adam all die, even so in Christ shall all be made alive. 23. But every man in his own order: Christ the first fruits; afterward they that are Christ's at His coming. 24. Then cometh the end, when he shall have delivered up the kingdom of God, even the Father; when he shall have put down all rule and all authority and power. 25. For he must reign, till he hath put all enemies under his feet. 26. The last enemy that shall be destroyed is death. (KJV)**

PUT DOWN YOUR WEAPON

We see so many times on the news how people are being shot and killed by the police and then, on many occasions, found not to be armed. It has become alarming and people are tired of seeing this, especially in the black communities. It is very difficult for the police officer to respond in such a violent society as ours. The adrenaline is pumped up, because you never know what the next person is going to do or how they are going to react to the police. Don't get me wrong here, I know that many of these shootings were not justified, but it is scary out there, and many police officers out there will not admit their fear. But in Paul's second letter to Timothy, Paul writes in **2 Timothy 1:7, For God hath not given us the spirit of fear; but of power, and of love, and of a sound mind. (KJV)** These words are to remind us all that God is there to protect us from all hurt, harm and danger. Stop and think when you are approached by a police officer. He may not be operating in the spirit of the lord, so you should be! Do not move; don't get out your car, don't make any gestures with your hands, don't argue or fuss, don't move! If the officer is wrong for detaining you, he will have to pay; but if you are wrong, well, deal with it and God will, no, God has already forgiven you!

I am reminded of an incident where I had to shoot. A police run came out in the early afternoon of a man walking down the street, pointing handgun at the houses. My partner that day was driving the scout car and we answered the call. As we turned onto the street in question, we could clearly see the man halfway down the block that matched the description. As we came closer, it was clear that he had a gun in his hand and was pointing it at every house. My partner, instead of stopping the scout car so that we could take cover, pulled right up to the subject and shouted out the window, "Hey you, drop that gun!" Well he did not drop the gun, instead, he turned towards us and raised the weapon as to fire at us. I dove into my partner's lap, upside down, and fired two shots at the subject. One of the shots took effect and knocked him down to the ground. We exited the scout car, found that the subject was shot in the side and arrested him. We then found that the weapon was a blank starter's pistol, but who would have known. The subject was a mental patient and was from a half way home in the area.

We took him to the Hospital where he was treated and no charges brought against him. Two days later, while sitting in the police mini station, I observed the same subject coming into the door. He walked up to my desk, pulled up his shirt, and said to me, "Look, some cop shot me". He then left the building. All I could say was thank you Jesus for your protection!

On another occasion, we were conducting a raid on where we just completed the buy of some major narcotics. The suspect was still inside as we continued surveillance of the home. As we entered the home and conducted our search, the suspect could not be found. We searched that house everywhere, knowing that there was no way he could have gotten out without being seen. Suddenly our sergeant, Gary Hendrix, said to all to be quite and listen. We could hear a sound, it was a snore! We followed the sound to the rafters above, and there he was. The suspect was lying in the rafters, on a 2x4 beam, with a loaded 12ga shotgun in his hands, and he was fast asleep. Had fear not taken over, he had the opportunity to fire on all of us, but fear made him sleep. God was protecting us again! We were in His hands, His mercy, and His grace! The suspect was apprehended without incident.

THE WORDS OF
MY MOUTH

Sometimes you have to think on a moment's notice. I can recall several times where I had to think fast and use the words of my mouth to get the job done. My partner and I were called to a family's home to assist with the commitment of their daughter to the psychiatric hospital. She was becoming very violent and they needed some help. As we entered the home, I witnessed a very large (around 400lbs) young lady, who was screaming at the top of her lungs, sweating profusely, slobbering, and was naked, no clothes on at all! When she turned and saw us, she became more violent and started turning furniture over. As she approached me, I had to react fast. I said to her, "hey beautiful, girl you are so fine. Are you ready for our date? I can't wait to take you out!" She paused and started to smile. I took her by the hand and told her that she had to get dressed so we could go to dinner.

The family had called EMS to transport, but I knew that she would not act right. So, I planned for her to ride in the scout car with me. I found her prettiest dress and told her that she would be the queen of the night. While continuing to sweet talk her, I got a brush and brushed her hair, sprayed some perfume on her, and kissed her forehead.

Without shoes on, I walked her to the scout car. When she saw the car, she got a little nervous. I convince her that she was getting VIP treatment and that this was her Limo. I got her in the back seat and then got back there with her. I had her head on my shoulder and I sweet talked her al the way to the hospital. She got nervous again when we arrived at the hospital, but I told her that we both had to checked out before we went to eat. I helped to get her on the stretcher and all went well. **Proverbs 25:11-13 (NKJV) reads, 11. A word fitly spoken is like apples of gold in settings of silver. 12. Like an earring of gold and an ornament of fine gold. Is a wise rebuker to an obedient ear. 13. Like the cold snow in time of harvest is a faithful messenger to those who sent him.**

There was another occasion I recall when the tongue saved me. I was laid-off from the police department for a while and was working security at a hospital. The hospital was small but it had two buildings across the street from one another. It was a Saturday night and my partner had called in sick, so I was working both building alone. It was a very busy night and people were all over, coming into the ER and across the street where the maternity ward was. As I was sitting at my desk, a very large Mexican male, who was obviously drunk stumbled in. He said he needed to use the bathroom. I directed him to the rest rooms at the bottom of the stairs. I had already become very agitated with so much that was going on that night that I had forgotten the drunk man. After about 45 minutes I realized that I never saw him leave, so I went down to make sure he had gone.

I knocked on the men's door and got no answer. The light was off, so I figured that he had gone. As I stated back upstairs, I realized that the light was on for the women's rest room. I knocked on the door to see if anyone was inside and the Mexican male shouted in a very angry voice, "WHAT". Oh, I got angry myself and shouted back, "GET YOUR A__ OUT OF THERE!" Suddenly the door came flying open and there he stood. A huge man, pants still down around his ankles, looking like he was ready to attack, with the biggest knife I had ever seen in his hands. He screamed at me, "WHAT DID YOU SAY?" Quickly, the words of my mouth that just got me in trouble had to get me out of trouble. I said to him, "Look at you, you come into my hospital, go to the lady's bathroom, drunk and out of order. But did you come to ask me if I wanted a drink, noooo you didn't even think about me!

He had a puzzled look on his face. He pulled up his pants, put the knife in it's sleeve, and said to me, "Well I tell you what, the next time I will come and get yo' a__! Then he left the building. I tell you what, I really could have used a drink after that!

23

MOSES AND I PARTED THE SEA

Exodus 23:20-22 (NKJV) 20. "Behold, I send an Angel before you to keep you in the way and to bring you into the place which I have prepared. **21.** "Beware of Him and obey His voice; do not provoke Him, for He will not pardon your transgressions; for My name is in Him. **22.** "But if you indeed obey His voice and do all that I speak, then I will be an enemy to your enemies and an adversary to your adversaries.

Not the Moses of biblical times but my partner Moses. We were called upon by a desperate neighbor in our scout car area. She explained that the drug dealers had taken over her rental property on Euclid street, and she was fearful for her life.

Moses and I did a little surveillance on the property and after viewing what we saw to be illegal narcotic activities, we took action. Moses went to the rear door and started banging on the door, yelling police! I went to the front door banging and yelling police! As the three young men inside ran towards the front door, which was a locked iron grate, The Lord gave me such strength, that as I grabbed the grate with both hands, I was able to pull the entire structure of the grate from the wall. The three men inside were so fearful, that they dropped their weapons and fell to the floor. No one was hurt, only by the grace of God!

God kept His angels watching over us time and time again. We were continuing to raid places that where drug houses belonging to a "family" called the Bones. They had gotten fed up with the way we were harassing them, so they made a plan to take us out. We received word that the next raid we conducted on their drug homes, we would be met by explosives. This information came from a very reliable source. We defied the warnings and conducted the raid. There was a bomb found on the scene, the bomb squad was called in, and the bomb was found to be a dud. We were able to finally shut this drug family down.

Psalm 91:11, God will command His Angles to protect you wherever you go. (CEV)

As a police officer one of our fundamental duties is to preserve evidence. In doing so we are faced with many obstacles and challenges. I recall on occasion where we conducted a raid on a drug house and the suspect inside ran into the bathroom and threw a large amount of rock cocaine into the toilet. The toilet was full of human feces and no water. I knew that in order to make a case, the cocaine had to be recovered. I found a small metal strainer, sat down on a milk crate, and fished out the cocaine bit by bit. Over two hundred rocks of cocaine were recovered which assisted us in making a good felony case against the suspect.

These are some of the things that are unseen by the public that the police go through. We are God's chosen few, chosen to enforce man's law, to protect man from himself, to be a helping hand, a listening ear, a shoulder to lean on; chosen to take on the world of criminal activity, to take the criminals off the street so that we can live worry free lives. The police are hated by those who want to be free to do whatever they want to disrupt the lives of the law abiding citizen. I pray that the law abiding citizens will come to love and respect the "Chosen Ones".

Let's talk a little about being chosen. I never wanted or even thought about becoming a law enforcement officer. The city of Detroit was doing a mass hiring of minorities. Police, Fire and EMS. So, since we, me and my friends, were looking for jobs, we put in the applications. We were called by the Detroit Fire Department first, but then decided to wait on the Police. Praise be to God, I answered His call and was able to do the good works that He called me to do. There were times when I was tempted to use my badge in the wrong way, but I knew that that was not what I was called to do. Oh, don't get me wrong, my life was not clean and squeaky, but I upheld the law of the land. I did wrong in my life, yes I was a sinner. I drank liquor, chased women, smoked, cussed, and all sorts of things before God woke something up inside of me. I knew that this calling as a Police Officer was preparing me for greater. **John 14: 12- Verily, verily, I say unto you, He that believeth on me, the works that I do shall he do also; and greater works than these shall he do; because I go unto my Father. (KJV)** As Jesus returned to the Father, the Holy Spirit was sent that gives us the power to perform greater works. The apostles were able to perform works such as Jesus did, but the Holy Spirit gave the power to not only heal, but to save souls.

God called me again to minister to the people of God, to use my experience as a police officer to tell how good He really is! The world is a dangerous place, but the Holy Spirit that lives in us, makes it possible for us to overcome the world through the grace and mercy of God! **1 John 4:4-Ye are of God, little children, and have overcome them: because greater is He that is in you, than he that is in the world. (KJV)**

There have been many times that God has protected me from this world's danger. I told you about some bombs and some shootings. There was so much more. When I first became a police officer, I walked a beat in one of the most dangerous neighborhoods in Detroit. It was called

"Woodward Beat 1". I was assigned to walk this beat with a rookie female officer on the afternoon shift. One evening as the sun went down, we were walking past an alley way when we herd gunshot blast, and pellets began to hit the ground at our feet. We were hired under, then Mayor Coleman Young's, affirmative Action plan. This plan was implemented in order to hire more minorities onto city services, the biggest was the Police Department. Well many of the white officers did not like this and were not very fond of the minorities that filled these positions, but like it or not, we were cops now, and we wore the same badge. When my beat partner and I took cover and called on the radio that we were under fire, the color of our skin did not matter. Police cars from three precincts and two other cities responded to make sure we were ok. This made me feel so special and I knew that this was the organization that I wanted to be a part of! Jesus says to the disciples **in John 16:32-33, "Behold, the hour cometh, yea, is now come, that ye shall be scattered' every man to his own, and shall leave me alone: and yet I am not alone, because the Father is with me. These things I have spoken to you, that in me ye might have peace. In the world ye shall have tribulation: but be of good cheer; I have overcome the world. (KJV)**

I was looking at Facebook one evening and I saw this poem about being a police officer. I do not know the author but it was so very true and I knew I had to share it with you.

TEARS OF A COP

(author unknown)

I have been where you fear to be.
I have seen what you fear to see.
I have done what you fear to do.
All these things I've done for you.
I am the one you lean upon.
The one you cast your scorn upon.
The one you bring your troubles to,
All these people I've been for you.

So yes, I cry when I think of some of these things that I have seen and witnessed. But I also know that it was God's will for me and so many others to be in the position to be that one to handle it. So I also rejoice in my days as a police officer, knowing that I was able to make a positive difference in this world. It was by the grace of God that I was able to do so. It was by the grace of God that I was saved from all hurt, harm and danger. It is by the grace of God that I am able to tell this story, that you may have a better understanding of what we, as police officers go through on a regular basis.

God called us to be what we are, protectors of human rights, enforcers of man's law, counselors, directors, deterrents, friends, a shoulder to lean on, an ear to hear your concerns, a smiling face, a helping hand. The man in blue that is there for you! Here are some more Police Officer poems:

POLICE OFFICER'S PRAYER

Lord, I ask for courage
Courage to face and
Conquer my own fears
Courage to take me
Where others will not go
I ask for strength of body
That I may protect others
....AMEN

A COP ON THE TAKE

by Wayne A. Linney

First, he takes the oath
Now look at all he takes,

He takes it in stride when people call him pig.
He takes time to stop and talk to children
He takes your verbal abuse while giving you a ticket you really deserve
He takes on creeps you would be afraid to even look at
He takes time away from his family to keep you safe
He takes your injured children to the hospital

ANOTHER POLICEMANS PRAYER

OH, ALMIGHTY GOD,
WHOSE GREAT POWER AND
ETERNAL WISDOM EMBRACES THE
UNIVERSE. WATCH OVER ALL POLICEMEN
AND LAW ENFORCEMENT OFFICERS.
PROTECT THEM FROM HARM IN THE PER-
FORMANCE OF THEIR DUTIES TO STOP CRIME,
ROBBERIES, RIOTS AND VIOLENCE WE PRAY.

WHAT ARE POLICE

"POLICE" – whether active, part time, or retired – are those who, at one point in their lives, wrote a blank check made payable to: "The City He or She Serves" for an amount of "up to AND including their life."

That is honor. And there are way too many people in this country today, who no longer understand that fact.

CLOSING STATEMENT

I loved being one of God's chosen few. The media does not share very much about the good things that police officers do. These things do not make good sensational news, but there are many more good things to know about policemen then there are bad! Policemen are human too and they have issues just like everyone else. Stop a cop every so often and talk to them, you will be amazed at how much they are just like you! We need your prayers, we need you help, we need your understanding. We are there for your good! God bless all law enforcement officers all over the world. AMEN!